Emergency Arabic

Mahmoud Gaafar

Series Editor: Jane Wightwick
Art Director: Mark Wightwick

Hippocrene Books, Inc.
New York

Emergency

Emergency

Arabic

CONTENTS

Arabic

⚡TAKE NOTE⚡

Traveling to a country where the language and culture are unfamiliar is exciting but can also be challenging. Often a smile and good manners will carry you a long way, and it helps to learn how to say at least "please" and "thank you."

When things are going smoothly on your trip you'll probably not notice the communication difficulties that can arise from a language barrier. Many people speak some English and will be happy to practice on you. But in more stressful situations, especially in remoter areas, you cannot always rely on English to make yourself understood or to get you out of a jam.

Emergency Arabic is designed for these situations. Carry it with you and use it to explain your situation clearly and to make polite requests. There's a pronunciation guide to help you say the words and phrases, or you can show the book to Arabic-speakers so that they can read it in their own language. There are even special "Answer Back" panels designed for them to point out an answer to your question.

So put **Emergency Arabic** in your pocket and travel light with confidence!

basics

KEY WORDS

yes	نعم ◆ na'am
no	لا ◆ laa
please	من فضلك ◆ min faDlak
thank you	شكراً ◆ shukran
hello	أهلا ◆ ahlan
goodbye	مع السلامة ◆ ma'as-salaama
where?	أين؟ ◆ aina
here	هنا ◆ huna
when?	متى؟ ◆ mataa
now	الآن ◆ al-aan
tomorrow	غداً ◆ ghadan
how much?	بكم؟ ◆ bikam
I don't understand	لا أفهم ◆ laa afham

basics

Down to

My name's...	◆ اسمي...	ismee
What's your name?	◆ ما اسمك؟	maa ismak
Pleased to meet you	◆ تشرفنا	tashar-rafna
Where are you from?	أنت من أين؟ ◆ anta min ain	
I'm American (fem.)	أنا أمريكي ◆ ana amreekeyy(a)	
I'm English (fem.)	أنا انجليزي ◆ ana ingleezeyy(a)	
I'm Canadian (fem.)	أنا كندي ◆ ana kanadeyy(a)	
I'm Scottish (fem.)	أنا اسكتلندي ◆ ana eskotlandeyy(a)	

Down to

basics

I'm Irish	أنا ايرلندي
(fem.)	◆ ana eerlandeyy(a)

I'm Welsh	أنا ويلزي
(fem.)	◆ ana wilzeyy(a)

I'm Australian	أنا أسترالي
(fem.)	◆ ana ostoraaleyy(a)

I now live in...	الآن أعيش في...
	◆ al-aan a'eesh fee

please point here ... أشر هنا من فضلك

please point here ...

أنا اسمي...	My name's...
أنا مصري	I'm Egyptian
أنا سوري	I'm Syrian
أنا مغربي	I'm Moroccan
أنا يمني	I'm Yemeni
أنا فلسطيني	I'm Palestinian

please point here ...

basics

my husband	زوجي ◆ zawjee
my wife	زوجتي ◆ zawjatee
my son	ابني ◆ ibnee
my daughter	ابنتي ◆ ibnatee
my mother	أمي ◆ um-mee
my father	أبي ◆ abee
my sister	أختي ◆ ukh-tee
my brother	أخي ◆ akhee
my father-in-law/ my mother-in-law	حماي / حماتي ◆ Hamaaya/ Hamaatee
my daughter-in-law/ my son-in-law	زوجة ابني / زوج بنتي ◆ zawjat ibnee/ zawj bintee
my family	أسرتي ◆ osratee
my relatives	أقربائي ◆ aqribaa'ee
my friend (masc.)/ fiancé	صديقي / خطيبي ◆ Sadeeqee/khaTeebee
my friend (fem.)/ fiancée	صديقتي / خطيبتي ◆ Sadeeqatee/khaTeebatee

basics

He is my partner/ She is my partner	هو شريكي /هي شريكتي ◆ huwa shareekee/ hiya shareekatee
I have two daughters	عندي ابنتين ◆ ana 'indee ibnatain
I have two sons	عندي ولدين ◆ 'indee waladain
My mother is here with us	أمي معنا هنا ◆ ummee ma'na huna

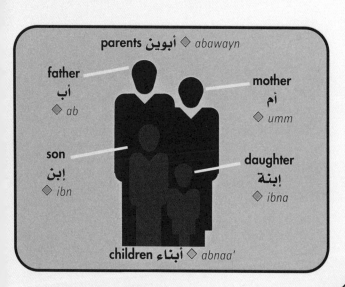

parents أبوين ◇ abawayn

father أب ◇ ab

mother أم ◇ umm

son إبن ◇ ibn

daughter إبنة ◇ ibna

children أبناء ◇ abnaa'

basics

KEY WORDS

bathroom	حمّام ◆ Ham-maam
bedroom	غرفة نوم ◆ ghorfat nawm
hot water	ماء ساخن ◆ maa' saakhin
toilet	تواليت ◆ tuwaaleet
sink	حوض ◆ HawD
faucet (tap)	صنبور ◆ Sunboor
drain	بالوعة ◆ baaloo'a
shower	دُش ◆ dosh-sh
bathtub	بانيو ◆ banyo
soap	صابون ◆ Saaboon
towel	منشفة ◆ minshafa
key	مفتاح ◆ miftaaH
lock	قفل ◆ qifl

to stay

door	باب ◆ baab
chair	كرسي ◆ korseyy
table	مائدة ◆ maa'ida
television	تليفزيون ◆ telivizyoon
light	نور ◆ noor
curtain	ستار ◆ setaar
bed	سرير ◆ sareer
blanket	بطانية ◆ baT-Taaneyya
pillow	وسادة ◆ wesaada
heater	مدفأة ◆ midfa'ah
air-conditioning	تكييف هواء ◆ takyeef hawaa'
crib (cot)	سرير أطفال ◆ sareer aTfaal
highchair	كرسي أطفال ◆ korseyy aTfaal

to stay

An extra blanket, please	بطانية إضافية من فضلك ◆ baT-Taaneyya iDaafeyya, min faDlak
Put the crib (cot) over there	ضع سرير الأطفال هناك ◆ Da' sareer al-aTfaal hunaak
We need soap and towels	نحتاج صابون ومناشف ◆ naHtaaj Saaboon wa manaashif
The air-conditioning doesn't work	تكييف الهواء لا يعمل ◆ takyeef al-hawaa' laa ya'mal
Can you repair the toilet?	ممكن تصلح التواليت ؟ ◆ momkin teSal-laH at-tuwaaleet
There's no hot water	لا يوجد ماء ساخن ◆ laa yawjad maa' saakhin
too hot/too cold	ساخنة جدا / باردة جدا ◆ saakhina jid-dan/ baarida jid-dan

to stay

The window is jammed shut	الشباك محشور لا يفتح
	◆ *ash-shubbaak maHshoor laa yaftaH*
My key is lost	مفتاحي ضاع
	◆ *miftaaHee Daa'*
How do we open this door?	كيف نفتح هذا الباب؟
	◆ *kaifa naftaH haazal baab*

please point here ... ... أشر هنا من فضلك

سنصلحه فورا	**We'll repair it right away**
سيأتي شخص ليساعدك	**Someone will come to help you**
سنحضره إلى غرفتكم	**We'll bring it to your room**
اتركها مع البواب	**Leave them with the doorman**
من فضلك اسأل الاستقبال	**Please ask reception**

please point here ... ... please point here ...

to stay

RENTING

kitchen	مطبخ ◈ maTbakh
living room	غرفة جلوس ◈ ghorfat joloos
dining room	غرفة طعام ◈ ghorfat Ta'aam
garbage	زبالة ◈ zebaala
electric meter	عداد ◈ 'ad-daad
deposit	تأمين ◈ ta'meen
inventory	قائمة ◈ qaa'ima
Where will we find the key?	أين سنجد المفتاح؟ ◈ aina sa-najid al-miftaaH

⚡TAKE NOTE⚡

Most rentals are long term. Short-term visitors will generally use hotels. In some resorts, however, you may rent a bungalow, a chalet, or an apartment.

to stay

Where do we leave the garbage?	أين نترك الزبالة؟ ◆ *aina natrok* *az-zebaala*
Where are the sheets/towels?	أين الملايات/المناشف؟ ◆ *ainal milaayaat/* *manaashif*
How much is the deposit?	كم قيمة التأمين؟ ◆ *kam qeemat* *at-ta'meen*
Will we pay for cleaning?	هل سندفع التنظيف؟ ◆ *hal sa-nadfa'* *at-tanZeef*

please point here ... أشر هنا من فضلك

المفاتيح في الاستقبال	The keys are at reception
سنقابلكم هناك	We'll meet you there
هذا سعره إضافي	You have to pay extra for that

please point here ...

أشر هنا من فضلك ...

to stay

PAYMENT

I'll need an invoice	سأحتاج فاتورة ◆ sa-aHtaaj fatoora
The invoice has a mistake	هناك خطأ في الفاتورة ◆ hunaak khaTa' fil fatoora
We didn't take this	لم نأخذ هذا ◆ lam na'khoz haaza
We only took one/two	أخذنا واحدة/اثنان فقط ◆ akhazna waaHida/ ithnaan faqaT
We didn't use the telephone	لم نستعمل التليفون ◆ lam nasta'mil at-telifoon
We didn't break this	لم نكسر هذا ◆ lam naksar haaza
We've paid for it	دفعنا ثمنه ◆ dafa'na thamanuh
Is the manager available?	المدير موجود؟ ◆ al-modeer mawjood

to stay

The total would be...

الإجمالي يكون...
◆ al-ijmaalee yakoon

Is this card acceptable?

هل هذا الكارت مقبول؟
◆ hal haazal kart maqbool

We only have traveler's checks.

معنا شيكات سياحية فقط
◆ ma'naa sheekaat siyaaHeyya faqaT

➤ **Page 47 for Numbers**

please point here ... أشر هنا من فضلك ...

دعني أسأل في الداخل	Let me ask inside
سنصلحها	We'll correct it
الفاتورة سليمة الآن	The invoice is correct now
خصمناه من التأمين	We deducted it from the deposit
لحظة، سأنادي المدير	One moment, I'll call the manager

please point here ... أشر هنا من فضلك ...

please point here ... أشر هنا من فضلك ...

to stay

KEY WORDS

map	خريطة	*khareeTa*
address	عنوان	*'unwaan*
street	شارع	*shaari'*
highway	طريق سريع	*Tareeq saree'*
distance	مسافة	*masaafa*
meter	متر	*mitr*
kilometer	كيلومتر	*kilomitr*
sign	علامة	*'alaama*
direction	اتجاه	*it-tijaah*
right	يمين	*yameen*
left	يسار	*yasaar*
straight on	على طول	*'ala Tool*
junction	تقاطع	*taqaaTo'*

Excuse me

we're lost!

corner	ناصية ◆ naaSiya
traffic light	إشارة مرور ◆ ishaarat moroor
traffic circle (roundabout)	دوران ◆ dawaraan
desert road	طريق صحراوي ◆ Tareeq SaHraaweyy
on foot	مشي ◆ masheyy
by car	بالسيارة ◆ bis-sayyaara
by bus	بالباص ◆ bil-baaS
by train	بالقطار ◆ bil-qiTaar
by boat/ferry	بالمركب/بالمعدية ◆ bil-markib/ bil me'ad-deyya
by plane	بالطائرة ◆ biT-Taa'ira

we're lost!

Excuse me!	**لو سمحت!** ◆ lau samaHt
Where's ...?	**أين...؟** ◆ aina
What street is this?	**أي شارع هذا؟** ◆ ayy shaari' haaza
What building is this?	**أي مبنى هذا؟** ◆ ayy mabna haaza
Where are we on the map?	**أين نحن على الخريطة؟** ◆ aina naHnu 'alal khareeTa
Which is the way there?	**أين الطريق إلى هناك؟** ◆ aina T-Tareeq ila hunaak
Is it far?	**هل هي بعيدة؟** ◆ hal hiya ba'eeda
Which is the easiest way?	**ما هي أسهل طريقة؟** ◆ maa hiya as-hal Tareeqa

سأدلكم على طريق سهل	I'll show you an easy way
إنها قريبة	It's close
إنها بعيدة	It's far
خذوا الباص	Take the bus
خذوا تاكسي أفضل	Better take a taxi
اتجه إلى اليمين	Turn right
اتجه إلى اليسار	Turn left
أول/ثاني/ثالث شارع	First/second/third street
على طول	Straight on
بعد أن تعبر...	After you cross...
اترك...	Go past...
أمام...	Opposite...

➡ Page 24 for landmarks

I'm a visitor	أنا زائر ◆ *ana zaa'ir*
I didn't know it was one-way	لم أعرف أنه اتجاه واحد ◆ *lam a'rif an-nu it-tijaah waaHid*
I don't read Arabic signs	أنا لا أقرأ لافتات بالعربية ◆ *ana laa aqra' lafitaat bil 'arabey-ya*
How much is the fine?	كم الغرامة؟ ◆ *kam al-gharaama*
Can I leave the car here?	ممكن أترك السيارة هنا؟ ◆ *momkin atrok as-say-yaara hona*

⚡TAKE NOTE⚡

Because they have foreigners in mind, traffic authorities will often erect street signs in both Arabic and English. If you're driving, try not to get distracted by funny spelling mistakes!

Broadly speaking, try always to expect the unexpected. The element of surprise keeps everyone on their toes. Honking is almost an involuntary activity, so don't take it too personally. It is not as forceful a statement as it may be in Europe or the US.

Excuse me

we're lost!

TRAFFIC INSTRUCTIONS

no entry
ممنوع الدخول
◆ mamnoo' ad-dokhool

no parking
ممنوع الانتظار
◆ mamnoo' lintiZaar

stop!
قف! ◆ qiff

slow down!
هدئ السرعة!
◆ had-di' as-sor'a

keep right!
الزم اليمين!
◆ ilzam al-yameen

keep left!
الزم اليسار!
◆ ilzam al-yasaar

pedestrians only
للمشاه فقط
◆ lil-moshaah faqaT

buses only
للباصات فقط
◆ lil-baaSaat faqaT

bicycle path
ممر للدراجات
◆ mamarr lid-dar-raajaat

crossing
عبور ◆ 'uboor

we're lost!

LANDMARKS

airport	مطار	maTaar
bank	بنك	bank
beach	شاطئ	shaaTi'
bridge	جسر	jisr
bus stop	موقف باصات	mawqaf baSaat
campsite	مخيم	mokhay-yam
castle	قلعة	qal'a
cave	كهف	kahf
temple	معبد	ma'bad
palace	قصر	qaSr
river	نهر	nahr
youth hostel	بيت الشباب	bait ash-shabaab

we're lost!

hotel	فندق	*funduq*
lake	بحيرة	*boHaira*
mountain	جبل	*jabal*
theater	مسرح	*masraH*
museum	متحف	*matHaf*
park	حديقة	*Hadeeqa*
parking lot (car park)	موقف سيارات	*mawqaf say-yaaraat*
school	مدرسة	*madrasa*
square	ميدان	*meedaan*
station	محطة	*maHaT-Ta*
mosque	مسجد	*masjid*
statue	تمثال	*timthaal*
market	سوق	*sooq*
university	جامعة	*jaami'a*

we're lost!

KEY WORDS

appointment	◆ maw'id موعد
doctor	◆ doktoor دكتور
dentist	دكتور أسنان ◆ doktoor asnaan
nurse	◆ momar-reDa ممرضة
ambulance	◆ is'aaf إسعاف
hospital	◆ mostashfa مستشفى
clinic	◆ 'iyaada عيادة
ward	◆ 'anbar عنبر
stretcher	◆ naq-qaala نقالة
operation	◆ jiraaHa جراحة
injury	◆ iSaaba إصابة
illness	◆ maraD مرض
insurance	◆ ta'meen تأمين

doctor!

examination	فحص	◆ faHS
test	اختبار	◆ ikhtibaar
prescription	روشتة	◆ roshet-ta
pharmacy	صيدلية	◆ Saydaley-ya
medicine	دواء	◆ dawaa'
pill	حبة	◆ Hab-ba
injection	حقنة	◆ Hoqna
syrup	شراب	◆ sharaab
ointment	مرهم	◆ marham
suppository	لبوس	◆ loboos
painkiller	مسكن	◆ mosak-kin
sedative	مهدئ	◆ mohad-di'
analysis	تحليل	◆ taHleel
x-ray	أشعة	◆ ashi'a

doctor!

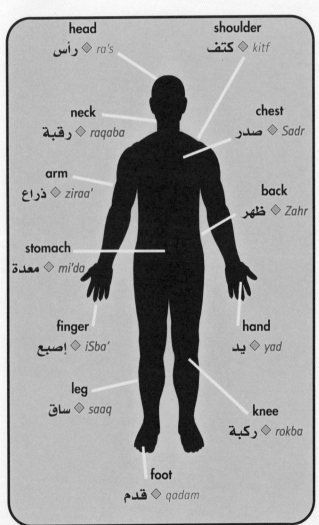

head	رأس	*ra's*
shoulder	كتف	*kitf*
neck	رقبة	*raqaba*
chest	صدر	*Sadr*
arm	ذراع	*ziraa'*
back	ظهر	*Zahr*
stomach	معدة	*mi'da*
finger	إصبع	*iSba'*
hand	يد	*yad*
leg	ساق	*saaq*
knee	ركبة	*rokba*
foot	قدم	*qadam*

doctor!

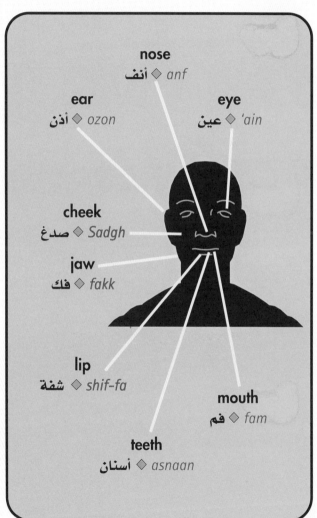

nose ◇ *anf* أنف

ear ◇ *ozon* أذن

eye ◇ *'ain* عين

cheek ◇ *Sadgh* صدغ

jaw ◇ *fakk* فك

lip ◇ *shif-fa* شفة

mouth ◇ *fam* فم

teeth ◇ *asnaan* أسنان

doctor!

The pain is here	الألم هنا ◆ al-alam huna
I can't move it	لا يمكنني أن أحركه ◆ laa yomkinonee an uHar-rikkuh
I have a headache	عندي صداع ◆ 'indee Sodaa'
I have a stomachache	عندي مغص ◆ 'indee maghaS
My back hurts	عندي ألم في ظهري ◆ 'indee alam fee Zahree
I feel sick	أشعر بالغثيان ◆ ash'or bil-ghathayaan
I have diarrhea	عندي إسهال ◆ 'indee is-haal

doctor!

استلق هنا	Lie down here
افتح فمك	Open your mouth
خذ نفس عميق	Breathe deeply
اسعل	Cough
ارفع هذا الكم	Roll up this sleeve
ارفع قميصك	Lift up your shirt
اثن ركبتيك	bend your knees

please point here ... أشر هنا من فضلك

⚡TAKE NOTE⚡

An accurate diagnosis may depend on the clarity and precision of what you say, and the ability of the doctor to understand exactly what you mean.

doctor!

I need a

Is it serious?	هل الأمر خطير؟ ◆ hal al-amr khaTeer
Is it infectious?	هل هو معد؟ ◆ hal huwa mo'di
Can it wait?	هل يمكنه الانتظار؟ ◆ hal yumkinuh al-intiZaar
I'll call our family doctor	سأتصل بطبيب العائلة ◆ sa'at-taSil bi-Tabeeb al-'aa'ila
Where's the nearest pharmacy?	أين أقرب صيدلية؟ ◆ aina aqrab Saydaley-ya
I will contact my insurer	سأتصل بشركة التأمين ◆ sa'at-taSil bi-sherikat at-ta'meen
I'm not insured	ليس عندي تأمين ◆ laisa 'indee ta'meen
Can I have a receipt?	ممكن تعطيني ايصال؟ ◆ momkin tu'Teenee eeSaal

I need a

doctor!

هل أنت مريض بالسكري؟	Are you diabetic?
إنها من أعراض ضربة الشمس	It's a symptom of sunstroke
عندك التهاب بسيط	You have a minor infection
أنا غير متأكد الآن	I'm not sure yet
أحتاج أن أراك مرة أخرى غدا	I need to see you again tomorrow
يجب أن تذهب إلى المستشفى	You have to go to the hospital
لا تتعرض للشمس	Keep out of the sun
اشرب ماء كثير	Drink plenty of water
خذ هذا الدواء	Take this medicine
قبل /بعد الوجبات	before/after meals
هل عندك حساسية؟	Are you allergic to anything?

doctor!

33

KEY WORDS

car	سيارة ◆ *say-yaara*
motorbike	دراجة نارية ◆ *dar-raaja naarey-ya*
bicycle	دراجة ◆ *dar-raaja*
boat	مركب ◆ *markib*
truck (lorry)	شاحنة ◆ *shaaHina*
donkey	حمار ◆ *Himaar*
driver	سائق ◆ *saa'iq*
bus	باص ◆ *baaS*
pedestrians	مشاه ◆ *moshaah*
child	طفل ◆ *Tifl*
dog	كلب ◆ *kalb*

an accident!

brakes	مكابح	makaabiH
animal	حيوان	Haywaan
tree	شجرة	shajara
ditch	حفرة	Hofra
curve	منحنى	monHana
flood	فيضان	fayaDaan
cell phone (mobile phone)	تليفون محمول	telifoon maHmool
public telephone	تليفون عام	telifoon 'aam
police	شرطة	shorTa
ambulance	إسعاف	is'aaf
fire engine	مطافي	maTaafee
rescue	إنقاذ	inqaaz
witness	شاهد	shaahid

an accident!

Come quickly!	تعال بسرعة!
	◆ ta'ala bi-sor'a
Someone is hurt	يوجد شخص مصاب
	◆ yewjad shakhS moSaab
Call an ambulance!	اطلب الإسعاف!
	◆ oTlob al-is'aaf
Where's a telephone?	أين التليفون؟
	◆ ain at-telifoon
Don't move him	لا تحركه
	◆ laa toHar-rikuh
It wasn't our fault	لم تكن غلطتنا
	◆ lam takun ghalTatna
They saw everything	هم شاهدوا كل شئ
	◆ hom shaahadu koll shai'
first aid	اسعافات أولية
	◆ is'aafaat aw-waley-ya

an accident!

Where did it happen?	أين وقع الحادث؟
Did anyone see it?	هل رآه أحد؟
We need to report it	يجب أن نبلغ عنه
Your license, please	رخصتك من فضلك
The insurance, please	التأمين من فضلك

please point here ... أشر هنا من فضلك ...

⚡TAKE NOTE⚡

Accidents are no fun anywhere in the world. All you can realistically be expected to do is prepare yourself as best you can by carrying a fire extinguisher, a first-aid box and a red reflective triangle. Try to keep a cool, clear head, stay at the scene and wait for the police.

trunk (boot)
صندوق ◇ *Sondooq*

taillight
ضوء خلفي
◇ *Daw' khalfee*

roof
سقف ◇ *saqf*

exhaust pipe
أنبوب العادم
◇ *anboob al-'aadim*

tire (tyre)
إطار ◇ *iTaar*

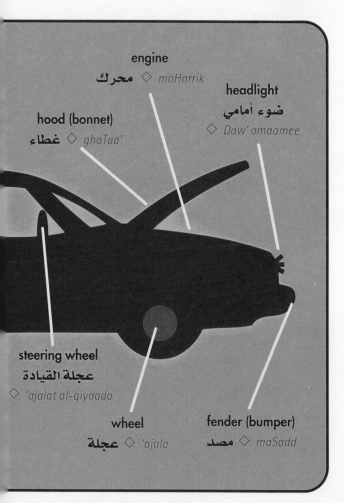

engine
محرك ◇ *moHarrik*

headlight
ضوء أمامي
◇ *Daw' amaamee*

hood (bonnet)
غطاء ◇ *ghaTaa'*

steering wheel
عجلة القيادة
◇ *'ajalat al-qiyaada*

wheel
عجلة ◇ *'ajala*

fender (bumper)
مصد ◇ *maSadd*

There's something wrong with it	هناك عطل فيها
	◆ *hunaak 'oTl feehaa*
The exhaust pipe is too loud	أنبوب العادم مزعج
	◆ *onboob al-'aadim muz'ij*
It's lost power	إنها بلا عزم
	◆ *in-nahaa bilaa 'azm*
The engine won't start	المحرك لا يدور
	◆ *al-muHar-rik laa yadoor*
The oil is leaking	الزيت يتسرب
	◆ *az-zait yatasar-rab*
It's overheating	إنها تسخن جدا
	◆ *in-nahaa taskhan jid-dan*
Can you repair it?	ممكن تصلحها؟
	◆ *momkin tuSaliH-haa*

an accident!

How long will it take?	كم تستغرق من الوقت؟ ◆ *kam tastaghriq min al-waqt*
What's the cost?	كم التكلفة؟ ◆ *kam at-taklifa*

أشر هنا من فضلك ... please point here

أنا ممكن أصلحها	I can repair it
ستكون جاهزة اليوم	It'll be ready today
ستكون جاهزة غدا	It'll be ready tomorrow
سأطلب قطعة الغيار	I'll order the part
لا يمكن تصليحها	It can't be repaired
ستتكلف...	It will cost...
على ضمانتي	I guarantee it

أشر هنا من فضلك ... please point here

KEY WORDS

savings account	حساب إدخار ◆ Hisaab id-dikhaar
current account	حساب جار ◆ Hisaab jaari
ATM (cash machine)	جهاز صرف تلقائي ◆ jihaaz Sarf tilqaa'eyy
bank	بنك ◆ bank
bill (note)	بنكنوت ◆ bankenoot
cash	نقدا ◆ naqdan
check (cheque)	شيك ◆ sheek
coin	عملة معدنية ◆ 'omla ma'daneyya
commission	عمولة ◆ 'omoola
credit card	بطاقة ائتمان ◆ biTaaqat i'timaan

talk

currency exchange	تغيير عملة ◆ taghyeer 'omla
exchange rate	سعر صرف ◆ si'r Sarf
form	استمارة ◆ istimaara
ID	تحقيق شخصية ◆ taHqeeq shakhSey-ya
money	مال ◆ maal
pin number	رقم سري ◆ raqam sir-reyy
signature	توقيع ◆ tawqee'
small change	فكة ◆ fak-ka
teller (cashier)	صرّاف ◆ Sar-raaf
transfer	تحويل ◆ taHweel
traveler's checks (traveller's cheques)	◆ شيكات سياحية sheekaat seyaaHey-ya
withdrawal	سحب ◆ SaHb

talk

Money

◀TAKE NOTE▶

Find out what you can from your bank about the local currency before you travel. US dollar traveler's checks are the recommended method of taking money. Cash machines are also widely available in most big cities.

I'd like to change…	أود أن أغيير...
	◆ awad an ughay-yir
What's the exchange rate?	ما هو سعر الصرف؟
	◆ maa huwa si'r aS-Sarf
I need to make a transfer	أود أن أقوم بتحويل
	◆ awad an aqoom bi-taHweel
How long will it take?	كم من الوقت يستغرق؟
	◆ kam min al-waqt yastaghriq
The machine won't accept it	الجهاز لا يقبله
	◆ aj-jihaaz laa yaqbaluh

talk

| The ATM has eaten my card | الجهاز التهم بطاقتي |
| | ◆ aj-jihaaz iltaham bi-Taaqatee |

| I've forgotten my pin number | نسيت رقمي السري |
| | ◆ naseet raqamee as-sirreyy |

please point here ... أشر هنا من فضلك

سأحتاج أن أرى جواز سفرك	I'll need to see your passport
ما هو رقم الحساب؟	What's the account number?
إذهب إلى شباك رقم...	Go to window number...
الإسم هنا مختلف	The name here is different
هذا ليس نفس التوقيع	This isn't the same signature

please point here ... أشر هنا من فضلك

talk

Money

SETTLING UP

check (bill)	الفاتورة ◆ al-fatoora
service charge	أجر الخدمة ◆ ajr al-khidma
sales tax	ضريبة المبيعات ◆ Dareebat al-mabee'aat
cover charge	كوفير ◆ koofair
tip	إكرامية ◆ ikraamey-ya
receipt	إيصال ◆ eeSaal
How much is this?	بكم هذا؟ ◆ bikam haaza
Is service included?	هل يشمل الخدمة؟ ◆ hal yashmal al-khidma
Is tax included?	هل يشمل الضريبة؟ ◆ hal yashmal aD-Dareeba

Money

talk

A receipt, please	إيصال من فضلك
	◆ *eeSaal min faDlak*
Keep the change	احتفظ بالباقي
	◆ *iHtafiZ bil-baaqi*

⚡TAKE NOTE⚡

A 10% tip is normal in a restaurant, unless you are particularly pleased, in which case you may leave more.

The principal is the same for taxi-drivers, tour guides, and similar locally-provided services.

Most upmarket restaurants and hotels will accept credit cards and include tax and service in the price. The numbers are likely to be printed in English.

In a more 'back-alley' place, you may wish to check beforehand whether it is a cash-only establishment.

talk

What's this amount for?	لم هذا المبلغ؟
	◆ *lima haazal mablagh*

The total isn't right	هناك خطأ في الإجمالي
	◆ *hunaak khaTa' fil-ijmaalee*

That's too expensive	هذا غال جدا
	◆ *haaza ghaali jid-dan*

I want to exchange this	أريد استبدال هذا
	◆ *oreed istibdaal haaza*

I want a refund	أريد استرجاع نقودي
	◆ *oreed istirjaa' noqoodee*

I want to see the manager	أريد أن أقابل المدير
	◆ *oreed an oqaabil al-modeer*

I don't have another card	ليس معي بطاقة أخرى
	◆ *laisa ma'ee biTaaqa okhra*

talk

I've forgotten
my wallet

نسيت حافظة نقودي
◆ naseet HaafiZat
noqoodee

أحتاج إلى طبعة من بطاقة الائتمان	I need an imprint of the credit card
لا نتعامل ببطاقات الائتمان	We don't accept credit cards
إذهب إلى الصرّاف	Go to the cashier
لا نتعامل بهذه البطاقة	We don't accept this card
سأعطيك فاتورة مفصلة	I'll give you an itemised invoice

➤ Page 16–17 for hotel/accommodation

talk

49

KEY WORDS

allergy	حساسية ◆ Hasaaseyya
calories	سعرات حرارية ◆ si'raat Haraareyya
diabetic	مريض بالسكري ◆ mareeD bis-sok-kareyy
diet	نظام تغذية ◆ niZaam taghzey-ya
fat	دهن ◆ dihn
food poisoning	تسمم ◆ tasam-mom
halal	حلال ◆ Halaal
ingredients	مكونات ◆ mokaw-winaat
intolerance to...	لا يتقبل... ◆ laa yataqab-bal
kosher	مباح لليهود ◆ mobaaH lil-yahood

I'm allergic

salt	ملح ◆ malH
sugar	سكر ◆ sok-kar
vegetarian	نباتي ◆ nabaateyy

⚡TAKE NOTE⚡

Lamb and chicken are probably the most popular meats in the Middle East. A vegetarian from a western country remains largely a novelty. But vegans are so unknown that the word doesn't even exist in the Arabic dictionaries.

Typically, Middle Eastern cuisine has no particular hang-ups about lashings of salt, bundles of white sugar, dollops of ghee, gallons of full-fat milk, or sacks of bleached white flour. It's where it all leads to that matters: dishes so delicious you have to have some more (and maybe diet it off when you get back home.)

To be fair, you can also buy lots of healthy, organic and unprocessed foods where you can taste the goodness.

I'm allergic

I have an allergy	عندي حساسية ◆ 'indee Hasaaseyya
I don't eat...	لا آكل... ◆ laa aakol
I don't like...	لا أحب... ◆ laa oHibb

➡ **Page 54–57 for types of food**

I'm vegetarian	أنا نباتي ◆ anaa nabaateyy
I'm diabetic	أنا مريض بالسكري ◆ anaa mareeD bis-sok-kareyy
What meat is this?	أي نوع لحم هذا؟ ◆ ayy naw' laHm haaza
Does this contain nuts?	هل يحتوي على مكسرات؟ ◆ hal yaHtawee 'ala mekas-saraat
Does this contain wheat?	هل يحتوي على قمح؟ ◆ hal yaHtawi 'ala qamH
Are you sure?	هل أنت واثق؟ ◆ hal anta waathiq

I'm allergic

to seafood!

Can we check with the chef?	ممكن نتأكد من الطباخ؟	◆ mumkin nit'ak-kid min aT-Tabaakh
The children always ask for it	الأطفال يطلبونه دائما	◆ al-aTfaal yaTloboonuh daa'iman

أشر هنا من فضلك ... please point here

ممكن نجهز طبق بدونه	We can prepare a dish without it
جرب هذا الطبق!	Try this dish!
آسف! لا يوجد شئ يناسبكم	Sorry, we have nothing suitable
دعني أسأل الطباخ	Let me ask the chef
أنا واثق أنه سيعجبكم	I'm sure you'll like it!
الأطفال لا يحبونه أبدا!	Kids never like it!

please point here ... أشر هنا من فضلك ...

to seafood!

FOOD FINDER

apple	تفاح ◈	tof-faaH
banana	موز ◈	mawz
beef	لحم بقري ◈	laHm baqareyy
carrot	جزر ◈	jazar
chicken	دجاج ◈	dajaaj
chili	شطة ◈	shaT-Ta
corn	ذرة ◈	dora
cucumber	خيار ◈	khiyaar
duck	بط ◈	baTT
fish	سمك ◈	samak
garlic	ثوم ◈	thawm
ginger	جنزبيل ◈	ganzabeel
goat	لحم ماعز ◈	laHm maa'iz
kidney	كلاوي ◈	kalaawi
lamb	ضأن ◈	Da'nee
lemon	ليمون ◈	laimoon
lentil	عدس ◈	'ads
liver	كبدة ◈	kibda

I'm allergic

to seafood!

English–Arabic

mushrooms	فطر	*fiTr*
nuts	مكسرات	*mekas-saraat*
onion	بصل	*baSal*
orange	برتقال	*bortoqaal*
peanuts	فول سوداني	*fool sudaaneyy*
pigeon	حمام	*Hamaam*
potato	بطاطس	*baTaaTis*
rabbit	أرانب	*araanib*
rice	أرز	*arozz*
seafood	مأكولات بحرية	*ma'koolaat baHrey-ya*
shrimp (prawns)	جمبري	*gambaree*
soybeans	فول صويا	*fool Soya*
strawberries	فراولة	*farawla*
thyme	زعتر	*za'tar*
tomato	طماطم	*TamaaTim*
veal	لحم بتلو	*laHm bitel-lo*

to seafood!

55

FOOD FINDER

'ads	عدس	lentil
araanib	أرانب	rabbit
arozz	أرز	rice
baSal	بصل	onion
baTaaTis	بطاطس	potato
baTT	بط	duck
bortoqaal	برتقال	orange
Da'nee	ضأن	lamb
dajaaj	دجاج	chicken
farawla	فراولة	strawberries
fiTr	فطر	mushrooms
fool Soya	فول صويا	soybeans
fool sudaaneyy	فول سوداني	peanuts
gambaree	جمبري	shrimp (prawns)
ganzabeel	جنزبيل	ginger
Hamaam	حمام	pigeon
jazar	جزر	carrot

to seafood!

Arabic–English

kalaawi	كلاوي	kidney
khiyaar	خيار	cucumber
kibda	كبدة	liver
laHm baqareyy	لحم بقري	beef
laHm bitel-lo	لحم بتلو	veal
laHm maa'iz	لحم ماعز	goat
laimoon	ليمون	lemon
ma'koolaat baHrey-ya	مأكولات بحرية	seafood
mawz	موز	banana
mekas-saraat	مكسرات	nuts
samak	سمك	fish
shaT-Ta	شطة	chili
TamaaTim	طماطم	tomato
thawm	ثوم	garlic
tof-faaH	تفاح	apple
za'tar	زعتر	thyme
dora	ذرة	corn

to seafood!

KEY WORDS

I've been robbed!	سرقوني ◆ saraqoonee	
thief	حرامي ◆ Haraameyy	
robbery	سرقة ◆ sariqa	
pick-pocket	نشال ◆ nash-shaal	
police	شرطة ◆ shorTa	
(police) station	القسم ◆ al-qism	
(police) report	محضر ◆ maHDar	
form	استمارة ◆ istimaara	
insurance	تأمين ◆ ta'meen	
suitcase	حقيبة سفر ◆ Haqeebat safar	
hand bag	حقيبة يد ◆ Haqeebat yad	
briefcase	حقيبة عمل ◆ Haqeebat 'amal	

thief!

camera	كاميرا ◆ *kamera*
car trunk (boot)	صندوق السيارة ◆ *Sondooq as-say-yaara*
cell phone (mobile phone)	محمول ◆ *maHmool*
computer	كمبيوتر ◆ *kombyootir*
earrings	حلق ◆ *Halaq*
ring	خاتم ◆ *khaatim*
necklace	عقد ◆ *'uqd*
bracelet	سوار ◆ *suwaar*
gold	ذهب ◆ *dahab*
diamond	الماس ◆ *al-maas*
watch	ساعة ◆ *saa'a*
passport	جواز سفر ◆ *jawaaz safar*

thief!

I want to report a theft	أريد أن أبلغ عن سرقة ◈ *oreed an ubal-ligh 'an sariqa*
I've lost...	◈ *faqadt* ...فقدت
I was attacked	هجموا علي ◈ *hajamoo 'aleyy*
I had put it in my bag	وضعتها في حقيبتي ◈ *waDa'tuhaa fee Haqeebatee*
It was taken from my pocket	أخذوها من جيبي ◈ *akhazoohaa min jaibee*
I left it in my room	تركتها في غرفتي ◈ *taraktoohaa fee ghorfatee*
This happened today	هذا حدث اليوم ◈ *haaza Hadath al-yawm*

thief!

It happened yesterday	هذا حدث أمس ◆ haaza Hadath ams
I need a copy of the police report	أحتاج صورة من المحضر ◆ aHtaaj Soora min al-maHDar

◥TAKE NOTE◤

Travelers in the Middle East have traditionally enjoyed 'honored guest' status. This probably has its roots in trips that lasted months on camel-back through deserts.

According to a religious and cultural code a 'passer-by' is entitled to certain privileges that used to include shelter, and today still do include protection and safe passage. If you think it's bad news for you to have something stolen, be sure it's a lot worse news for the thief if he gets caught.

A sure way of ruining your trip is losing or misplacing an important item. Most people will head straight for their consulates, but sometimes this is not possible and they have to report the incident to the local police.

thief!

DESCRIBING ITEMS

new	جديد ◆ jadeed
old	قديم ◆ qadeem
big	كبير ◆ kabeer
small	صغير ◆ Sagheer
black	أسود ◆ aswad
blue	أزرق ◆ azraq
brown	بني ◆ bon-nee
green	أخضر ◆ akhDar
orange	برتقالي ◆ bortoqaalee
pink	وردي ◆ wardee
purple	بنفسجي ◆ banafsajee
red	أحمر ◆ aHmar
white	أبيض ◆ abyaD
yellow	أصفر ◆ aSfar

thief!

leather	جلد ◆ *jild*
valuable	قيم ◆ *qay-yim*
immitation	تقليد ◆ *taqleed*
authentic	أصلي ◆ *aSlee*
antique	تحفة ◆ *toHfa*

please point here ... أشر هنا من فضلك

ماذا فقدت؟	What's missing?
ما لونه؟	What color was it?
ما قيمته؟	How much was it worth?
هل اسمك عليه؟	Did it have your name on it?

أشر هنا من فضلك ... please point here

please point here ... أشر هنا من فضلك

thief!

DESCRIBING PEOPLE

man
◇ rajol رجل

woman
إمرأة ◇ imra'ah

glasses
نظارة ◇ naZ-Zaara

short hair
شعر قصير
◇ sha'r qaSeer

long hair
شعر طويل
◇ sha'r Taweel

moustache
شوارب
◇ shawaarib

beard
لحية ◇ liHya

about ... years old حوالي...عاما
◇ Hawaaleyy...'aaman

thief!

tall	طويل ◆	*Taweel*
short	قصير ◆	*qaSeer*
fat	سمين ◆	*sameen*
thin	نحيل ◆	*naHeel*
old	مسن ◆	*mos-sinn*
young	شاب ◆	*shaabb*

please point here ... أشر هنا من فضلك ...

املاء هذه الاستمارة	Fill out this form
وقع هنا	Sign here
سننظر في الأمر	We'll look into it
وجدناها!	We've found it!
سأحضر شخصا يتكلم الانجليزية	I'll get someone who speaks English
مسؤول الأمن سيتولى الموضوع	The security officer will deal with it

please point here ...

أشر هنا من فضلك ...

thief!

KEY WORDS

arrested	مقبوض عليه ◆ maqbooD 'alaih
attorney (lawyer)	محام ◆ moHaami
bail	كفالة ◆ kafaala
charge	تهمة ◆ tohma
consulate	قنصلية ◆ qonSoley-ya
court	محكمة ◆ maHkama
defense	دفاع ◆ difaa'
deportation	ترحيل ◆ tarHeel
embassy	سفارة ◆ sifaara
fine	غرامة ◆ gharaama
interpreter	مترجم ◆ motarjim
judge	قاض ◆ qaaDee
law	قانون ◆ qaanoon

# of trouble

legal	قانوني ◈ *qanooneyy*
(police) officer	ضابط ◈ *Daabit*
(police) station	قسم ◈ *qism*
prison	سجن ◈ *sijn*
prosecution	إدعاء ◈ *id-di'aa'*
statement	أقوال ◈ *aqwaal*
suspect	متهم ◈ *mot-taham*
warning	إنذار ◈ *inzaar*
possession	حيازة ◈ *Hiyaaza*
smuggling	تهريب ◈ *tahreeb*
narcotics	مخدرات ◈ *mokhad-diraat*
stolen goods	بضائع مسروقة ◈ *baDaa'i masrooqa*

Keeping out

I apologise	◈ أنا آسف	anaa aasif
I'm just visiting	◈ أنا زائر	anaa zaa'ir
It wasn't me	◈ ليس أنا	laisa ana
I don't understand	◈ لا أفهم	laa afham
I can't read this	لا أستطيع أن أقرأ هذا ◈	laa astaTee' an aqra' haaza
I didn't know it's forbiddden	لم أكن أعرف أنه ممنوع ◈	lam akon aa'rif an-nuh mamnoo'
Is he under arrest?	هل هو مقبوض عليه؟ ◈	hal huwa maqbooD 'alaih

Keeping out

Do we need to remove our shoes?	هل نخلع الأحذية؟ ◈ *hal nakhla' al-aHzeya*
Are they fasting?	هل هم صائمين؟ ◈ *hal hom Saa'meen*
Are these clothes suitable?	هل هذه الملابس مناسبة؟ ◈ *hal haazihil malaabis monaasiba*

please point here ... أشر هنا من فضلك

هذا غير قانوني	That's illegal
سأعطيك إنذار هذه المرة	I'll just warn you this time
يجب أن تدفع الغرامة	You have to pay the fine
أين جواز سفرك؟	Where's your passport?
يجب أن تأتي معي إلى القسم	You have to come with me to the station

please point here ... أشر هنا من فضلك

Keeping out

| Can I call the ... | ممكن اتصل ... |
| | ◆ momkin at-taSil |

| American embassy? | بسفارة أمريكا |
| | ◆ bi-sifaarit amreeka |

| British embassy? | بسفارة بريطانيا |
| | ◆ bi sifaarit biriTanya |

| Canadian consulate? | قنصلية كندا |
| | ◆ qonSoley-yat kanada |

| I need an English-speaking lawyer | أريد محام يتكلم انجليزي |
| | ◆ oreed moHaami yetkal-lam ingeleezeyy |

| I have to contact my family | يجب أن أتصل بأسرتي |
| | ◆ yajib an at-taSil bi'osratee |

| I need to make a phone call | أريد أن أتصل بالتليفون |
| | ◆ oreed an at-taSil bit-tilifoon |

| I don't know anything about it | لا أعرف عنه شيء |
| | ◆ laa 'araf 'anuh shai' |

Keeping out

of trouble

I can't say
anything yet

لا أقدر أن أقول شيئا الآن
◆ laa aqdar an aqool
shai'an al-aan

هل لديك أقوال؟	Do you want to make a statement?
هل تريد أن تتصل بالتليفون؟	Do you want to make a phone call?
هذه حقوقك	These are your rights
المترجم سيأتي الآن	The interpreter is coming now
أسرتك هنا	Your family is here
لا تخافوا، أنتم في أمان هنا	Don't be afraid, you're safe here

please point here ...

Keeping out

⚡TAKE NOTE⚡

Away from home, it makes good sense to be even more careful than you usually are. It is worth remembering that what is illegal at home will most likely be illegal everywhere else too.

Although we hope it won't happen, it is possible that you may find yourself, unintentionally, in trouble with the law. Do not compound the problem by behaving in an arrogant fashion or by being rude, especially to the police. Try to cope with the pressure of the situation, and remember that as a foreign national, your consulate will have to get involved at some point.

What are you charging me with?	ما هي تهمتي؟
	◆ *maa hiya tohmati*

How much is the fine?	كم الغرامة؟
	◆ *kam al gharaama*

Can I post bail?	ممكن أدفع كفالة؟
	◆ *momkin adfa' kafaala*

# of trouble

Will I stand trial?

هل ستحاكموني؟
◈ *hal sa-toHaakimoonee*

How long do I have to stay here?

إلى متى سأظل هنا؟
◈ *ilaa mataa sa'aZall huna*

لن نتهمك بشئ	**We won't be charging you**
تفضل، مع السلامة	**You're free to go**
يجب أن تعود إلينا	**You need to come back**
اترك جواز سفرك	**Leave your passport**
نريدك أن ترد على بعض الأسئلة	**We want you to answer some questions**

please point here ...

73

NUMBERS

one	واحد ◆	*waaHid*
two	اثنان ◆	*ithnaan*
three	ثلاثة ◆	*thalaatha*
four	أربعة ◆	*arba'a*
five	خمسة ◆	*khamsa*
six	ستة ◆	*sit-ta*
seven	سبعة ◆	*sab'a*
eight	ثمانية ◆	*thamanya*
nine	تسعة ◆	*tis'a*
ten	عشرة ◆	*'ashra*
eleven	إحدى عشر ◆	*iHda 'ashar*
twelve	اثنا عشر ◆	*ithna 'ashar*
thirteen	ثلاثة عشر ◆	*thalaath 'ashar*
fourteen	أربعة عشر ◆	*arba'at 'ashar*
fifteen	خمسة عشر ◆	*khamsat 'ashar*
sixteen	ستة عشر ◆	*sit-tat 'ashar*
seventeen	سبعة عشر ◆	*sab'at 'ashar*
eighteen	ثمانية عشر ◆	*thamaniyat 'ashar*
nineteen	تسعة عشر ◆	*tis'at 'ashar*

reference

twenty	عشرين ◆ 'ishreen
twenty-one	واحد وعشرين ◆ waaHid wa 'ishreen
twenty-two	اثنان وعشرين ◆ ithnaan wa 'ishreen
thirty	ثلاثين ◆ thalaatheen
forty	أربعين ◆ arba'een
fifty	خمسين ◆ khamseen
sixty	ستين ◆ sitteen
seventy	سبعين ◆ sab'een
eighty	ثمانين ◆ thamaneen
ninety	تسعين ◆ tis'een
one hundred	مئة ◆ mi'a
one thousand	ألف ◆ alf

⚡TAKE NOTE⚡

Although you will find western numbers used in the Middle East, Arabic also has its own set of figures:

٠	١	٢	٣	٤	٥	٦	٧	٨	٩
0	1	2	3	4	5	6	7	8	9

What's the time? كم الساعة؟
◈ kam as-saa'a

It's two o'clock الساعة اثنين
◈ as-saa'a ithnain

`11:00` الساعة إحدى عشرة
◈ as-saa'a iHda 'ashar

`11:15` الساعة إحدى عشرة وربع
◈ as-saa'a iHda 'ashar
wa rub'

`14:30` اثنين ونصف
◈ ithnain wa niSf

`14:45` ثلاثة إلا ربع
◈ thalaatha il-la rub'

reference

Monday	الأثنين ◆ al-ithnain
Tuesday	الثلاثاء ◆ ath-thulaathaa'
Wednesday	الأربعاء ◆ al-arbi'aa'
Thursday	الخميس ◆ al-khamees
Friday	الجمعة ◆ aj-jum'a
Saturday	السبت ◆ as-sabt
Sunday	الأحد ◆ al-aHad
now	الآن ◆ al-aan
soon	قريبا ◆ qareeban
today	اليوم ◆ al-yawm
yesterday	أمس ◆ ams
tomorrow	غدا ◆ ghadan

reference

MONTHS

January	يناير ◆ yanaayir
February	فبراير ◆ febraayir
March	مارس ◆ maaris
April	أبريل ◆ abreel
May	مايو ◆ maayo
June	يونيو ◆ yoonyo
July	يوليو ◆ yoolyo
August	أغسطس ◆ aghostos
September	سبتمبر ◆ sibtimbir
October	أكتوبر ◆ octobir
November	نوفمبر ◆ novimbir
December	ديسمبر ◆ deesimbir

What's today's date?
◆ maa huwa tareekh al-yawm ما هو تاريخ اليوم؟

It's June 12
١٢ يونيو
◆ ithna 'ashar yoonyo